TURKEY COOKBOOK

Healthy Recipes for the Year 'Round

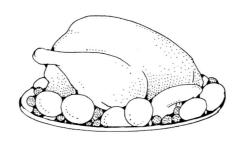

Judi & Tony Meisel

Photographs by Lionel Martinez

SMITHMARK

This edition published in 1993 by
SMITHMARK Publishers Inc.
16 East 32nd Street, New York, NY 10016

SMITHMARK books are available for bulk purchase
for sales promotion and premium use.
For details write or call the manager of special sales,
SMITHMARK Publishers Inc.,
16 East 32nd Street, New York, NY 10016; 212-532-6600.

Produced by AM Publishing Services
227 Park Avenue, Hoboken, NJ 07030
and
Wieser & Wieser, Inc.
118 East 25th Street, New York, NY 10010

Pottery courtesy of The Doofpot, Greenport, NY

Origination and Printing: Regent Publishing Services Ltd.

Printed in Hong Kong

10 9 8 7 6 5 4 3 2 1

ISBN 0-8317-8296-X

INTRODUCTION

Benjamin Franklin thought the turkey should have been proclaimed our national bird, being of a more kindly and less warlike disposition than the eagle. Also much better to eat, he might have added. For years, turkeys have been the celebratory bird of choice in America: Christmas, Thanksgiving, New Year's Day—feasts of autumnal abundance and large family gatherings., crackling fires and mulled wine.

But times change, and with them diets and gatherings change also. Few of us indulge the way our forefathers did, and few of us can conjure up families by the dozens. The turkey has changed, too. Not, mind you, on its own. Careful breeding and farming procedures have made the modern bird, heavier in the breast, leaner, more tender and succulent. And our preoccupation with lighter, less fatty foods has made the new turkey an ideal centerpiece for meals, from breakfast hash to a grand set piece at a formal dinner.

Furthermore, turkey can be bought whole (in varying sizes), in parts, smoked, as rolled boneless breasts and as cutlets. It can be frozen. It can be roasted, fried, braised, poached, baked and barbecued. It can be turned into soups, salads, mousses, scaloppine, sauces, fricassees, pies, hashes, aspics and more. And, like other white meats, it takes on the flavors of what it's cooked with. Tomatoes and oregano give it Italian flavor, ginger and soy sauce transform it into oriental splendor.

Herein are a number of unusual and enticing recipes for our native bird. And give thanks that we have such a splendid object for our culinary experimentation.

Judi and Tony Meisel
New Suffolk, NY

ROAST TURKEY

Roasting a turkey is the bane of Thanksgiving and Christmas. Too often it comes out dry and tough, and generally lacking in savor. There are as many methods to roasting a bird as there are cooks, but the following is one we have found to be almost fool-proof. It demands attention, and is untraditional in that the stuffing is cooked separately, thereby lessening the chance of spoilage or food poisoning. The lemons and onions inside the bird add moisture and flavor.

1 fresh-killed turkey, 12-14 pounds, dressed
2 large onions, peeled and cur into quarters
2 lemons, cut into quarters
1 cup (1/2 lb.) unsalted butter, at room temperature
1 tablespoon chopped garlic
1 tablespoon chopped fresh herbs (parsley, tarragon, chervil, thyme, alone or in combination)
2 teaspoons freshly ground black pepper
salt to taste

Clean the turkey, removing excess fat and any remaining pin feathers. Dry thoroughly. Place the onions and lemons in the large cavity. Mix the softened butter, chopped garlic, herbs and pepper and coat the Turkey, working as much under the skin as possible and placing about 1/4 cup in the cavity. Sew-up or skewer closed the bird. Tie the legs together with twine. Preheat the oven to 325 degrees. Place the turkey on a rack in a large roasting tin, breast up. Place in the oven and roast for about 3 hours (ca. 15 minutes per lb., basting with the pan juices every 15 minutes. If the breast starts to get too dark, cover it with a foil tent (removing this 15 minutes before the turkey is done. To test for doneness, pierce the thickest part of the thigh with a skewer. If the juices run clear, the turkey is done. If they run red, continue to cook, testing every 15 minutes. When done, remove the turkey to a platter and let stand for 10-15 minutes before carving. This will make for firmer meat and finer flavor. Salt only at this time. Salting before cooking can make for a dry bird. The lemons and onions can be discarded or used later for a piquant hash. Serve with pan gravy (see below) and any vegetables or stuffing you prefer. Our favorite is the rice stuffing following.

RICE STUFFING

So many bread stuffings are heavy and soggy, we experimented with eastern pilafs and came up with this. Do not use quick-cooking rice or brown rice. The first will crumble, the second will make too heavy a dish.

2 cups long grain rice
1/2 cup unsalted butter
1 onion, chopped
1 cup sliced mushrooms
1 clove garlic, chopped
1/2 cup pine nuts
1/2 cup dried apricots, coarsely chopped
1/4 cup dried currants
salt and freshly ground black pepper to taste

Fill a large pan with water. Salt it and bring to a boil. Add the rice, return to a boil, lower the heat to medium and cook until tender, about 12 minutes if the rice is the new crop. Drain. Rice stays fluffier if cooked like pasta. In the same pot, melt the butter, add the onions, mushrooms and garlic and sauté until lightly golden. Add the apricots and currents and simmer for five minutes. Fold in the rice and toss well to coat with the butter mixture. Either serve immediately, or pack into a covered casserole and keep warm in a low oven until dinner. It will stay moist and buttery for as long as 2-3 hours.

PAN GRAVY

The traditional gravy for turkey is viscous and pasty. Following the French, we like this one better.

turkey giblets (minus the liver)
2 cups water
1 carrot, chopped coarsely
1 stick celery
1 small onion
1/2 cup dry white wine, Madeira or vermouth

Clean the giblets and cut them into small pieces. In a small saucepan, place the giblets, carrot, celery and onion. Pour in the water. Bring to a boil, skimming the froth from the surface. When the liquid is clear, reduce the heat and simmer for 30 minutes, uncovered, or until reduced by half. Let cool slightly, then pour all into a food processor and puree. Set aside. When the turkey if out of the oven and resting in its platter, pour the wine or other liquid into the roasting pan placed on top of the stove over high heat. Let it bubble up, stirring with a wooden spoon all the time. Be sure to scrape up all the brown bits on the bottom. Remove from the heat and skim some (not all) the fat from the gravy. Add the puree to the pan, heat up, and serve.

LOW-FAT ROAST TURKEY

Instead of coating and basting the turkey with butter, use either olive oil or margarine. Both will produce a different taste, however, and extra herbs or flavorings may be used with discretion (grated orange or lemon peel adds a nice touch). The stuffing, likewise, can stand the substitution of margarine for butter, but do not salt it as margarine tends to be high in sodium, unless specifically noted otherwise on the package.

TURKEY VEGETABLE SOUP

Instead of the usual, try this refreshing mixture for a hearty one-dish meal. The shredding of the vegetables is easy using a food processor and the shredding disc.

4 quarts turkey stock, canned or fresh
2 cups cooked turkey, diced
3 tablespoons unsalted butter
1 large onion, thinly sliced
1 leek, white part only, shredded
1 carrot, shredded
3 cups Napa or Savoy cabbage,
*   shredded*
1 cup snow peas, shredded
2 sprigs fresh mint
2 springs fresh basil
salt and pepper to taste

Heat the stock gently. Add the turkey. In another large pot, melt the butter and gently sauté the onion, leek and carrot until soft. Add this mixture to the stock. Add the cabbage, snow peas, mint, basil and salt and pepper to the stock, cover and simmer for 20 minutes. Serve with grated cheese on the side. Serves 4-6.

TURKEY CUTLETS

Turkey cutlets, or slices from the breast, make quick and relatively inexpensive entrées. Either buy a whole breast and cut them yourself, or buy them precut and packaged.

The easiest method of cooking cutlets is to sauté them in oil or butter for 10 minutes, turning them once, and then add flavorings and liquid to the pan, cover it and simmer until tender. The cutlets can be floured or dipped in beaten egg and bread crumbs first, but for lightness and low calories, plain is fine. Allow 1–1 1/2 pounds for four people.

Following are a number of variations on the cutlet theme, each for 4 servings:

TURKEY MEXICAN
Add 2 chopped tomatoes, 2 tablespoons of chopped chilies, 1 chopped onion to the pan. Cover and cook for 10 minutes.

TURKEY MARSALA
Add 1 cup sliced, sautéed mushrooms and 1/4 cup Marsala wine to the pan. Cover and cook for 10 minutes.

TURKEY CALIFORNIA
Add 4 cubed artichoke bottoms, 1 chopped onion, 1 chopped tomato to the pan. Cover and cook 5 minutes.

TURKEY NORMAN
For this variation, use butter. Add 1/4 cup Calvados or apple brandy to the pan and flame. When the flames die down, add 1/2 sweet apple, cubed and 1/2 cup heavy cream. Cover and cook for 5 minutes.

TURKEY SCALLOPINE

With the price of veal what it is, turkey offers an inexpensive, and equally delicious, alternative.

1 pound turkey breast in one piece
1/2 cup flour
4 tablespoons unsalted butter
2 tablespoons olive oil
1/2 cup grated Parmesan cheese
1 lemon
1/2 teaspoon freshly ground black pepper

Freeze the turkey breast for one hour. Remove from freezer and, using a very sharp knife, slice the breast lengthwise into 1/4-inch slices. Cover each slice individually with wax paper and pound gently with a flat mallet or rolling pin until the slices are about 1/8-inch in thickness.

Dredge the slices in flour and melt the butter mixed with oil in a large skillet or sauté pan. Over medium heat, sauté the turkey slices until lightly browned on both sides. Arrange them in a fireproof baking dish, squeeze lemon juice over them and sprinkle with the Parmesan cheese and pepper. Pour the pan juices over and bake in a 350 degree oven for 15 minutes until the cheese is melted and the surface browned. Makes 4 servings.

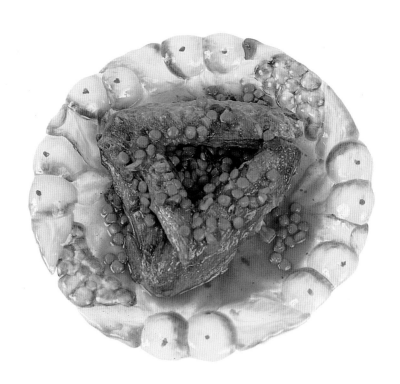

BRAISED WINGS
WITH LENTILS

Turkey wings are usually a good buy in parts. For those who like to pick and chew, they can make a juicy and succulent meal. However, since they are virtually devoid of fat, long, slow braising will add moisture and flavor, as well as tenderizing them.

2 tablespoons butter or margarine
1 large onion, chopped
1 large carrot, chopped
1 stick celery, chopped
4 wings
2 cups chicken broth (canned, salt-free, is ok)
2 cups cooked lentils
1/2 teaspoon dried thyme
1 teaspoon black pepper

In a heavy casserole with a tight-fitting lid, melt the butter or margarine. Sauté over medium heat the onion, carrot and celery until soft, about 10 minutes. Add the wings and brown gently, turning often, about 10 minutes more (the wings can be skinned or not, as you prefer). Add the stock, lentils, thyme and pepper and cover the casserole. Turn heat to low and let simmer for about 1 1/2 hours or until tender. Remove the wings to a warm serving platter. Turn up the heat under the casserole and let the juices cook down until reduced by half. Pour over the wings and serve with either buttered noodles or plain boiled potatoes and a simple green salad. Serves 4.

HOT TURKEY SANDWICHES

Hot turkey sandwiches are an old diner standby, but you can do better than that!

2 tablespoons butter or margarine
1 1/2 level tablespoon flour
2 1/2 cups hot turkey broth
1/4 teaspoon ground nutmeg
salt and pepper to taste
leftover sliced turkey, at room temperature
8 slices firm white bread

In a saucepan, melt the butter over low heat. Sprinkle the flour in pan and blend well with a wooden spoon. Allow to cook for 2-3 minutes, constantly stirring to get rid of the raw flour taste. gradually add the hot broth, stirring all the time until well-blended. Add the nutmeg and salt and pepper and cover the pan, letting the sauce cook gently for 10 minutes. Arrange four slices of bread on four plates. Cover with sliced turkey in whatever quantity and proportions of white to dark meat you prefer. Top with the other slices of bread. When ready to serve, pour equal amounts of hot gravy over all and let stand a few minutes for the gravy to be soaked up and the bread to be warmed. Serve with mashed potatoes and cranberry sauce. Serves 4.

TURKEY
TONNATO

Vitello tonnato—veal with tuna sauce—is one of
the classic summer specialties of Piedmont in
northern Italy. Made with turkey, it is just as
delicious, lower in fat and a lot cheaper. In
Italy, this is usually served as an antipasto,
but it makes a splendid light meal with a
salad and good, crusty bread.

1 1/2 cups yogurt or mayonnaise
1 tablespoon lemon juice
1 7-ounce can tuna in oil, mashed
1 clove garlic, chopped
1 teaspoon capers, chopped
2 anchovy filets, chopped (optional)
roast turkey breast, enough for 6 people

Combine the mayonnaise, lemon juice,
tuna, garlic, capers and anchovy, whisking well. Spread over the sliced turkey in
a deep dish or platter and let rest for at
least 2 hours. If preferred, it may be covered with plastic wrap or foil and refriger-
ated overnight. Just make sure that you let it
warm up to room temperature before serving.
Serves 6.

TURKEY BOLOGNESE

Another variation on a classic Italian specialty. This makes a very rich and filling dinner entrée.

6 slices of turkey breast, 1/4-inch thick
salt and pepper
flour
*   4 tablespoons sweet butter*
*   6 slices prosciutto or baked ham*
*   1 lb. sliced mushrooms, sautéed in 2 tablespoons butter*
*   1 cup grated Parmesan cheese*
*   1/2 cup chicken or turkey broth*

Salt and pepper the turkey slices and coat them lightly with flour. Melt the butter n a large, heavy skillet or sauté pan over low heat. Add the turkey slices and cook very gently for about 5 minutes on each side. Place a slice of ham on each turkey slice, then a layer of mushrooms and finally 2 generous tablespoons of Parmesan over each. Moisten the layered turkey slices with a tablespoon of broth for each and cover the pan. Continue to cook over low heat for another 10 minutes. The cheese, butter and broth form a rich sauce and the turkey will be permeated with the flavors of ham, mushrooms and cheese. Serve immediately. Serves 6.

TURKEY HASH

One of the grand, old recipes for a hearty cold weather breakfast, turkey hash makes a good centerpiece for an elegant brunch or supper party.

4 strips bacon, diced
4 cups diced, cooked turkey
2 onions, chopped
6 boiled potatoes, cubed
1/2 teaspoon ground nutmeg
1/2 teaspoon black pepper
1 teaspoon salt
1/2-1 cup heavy cream (optional)

In a large frying pan, sauté the bacon until crisp. Remove the bacon with a slotted spoon and set aside. Add the onions to the pan and sauté until soft and lightly browned. Add the turkey and potatoes, the nutmeg and salt and pepper. Mix well and press down. Cook over medium heat until hot through and crusty on the bottom, about 10-15 minutes. If you wish a crustier has, you can mix the ingredients again and press down again, letting a second crust form. As a final gilding, add 1/2-1 cup heavy cream after the crust has formed and heat gently. Serve as is or topped with a fired or poached egg for each serving. Serves 6.

POACHED TURKEY WITH SALSA VERDE

Poached turkey stays juicy and tender, but it must cook very slowly. This can be prepared a day before serving.

6 slices turkey breast, cut 1/2-inch thick
4 cups water
1 onion stuck with 2 cloves
1 stick celery
1 carrot, cut in chunks
1 teaspoon crushed black peppercorns
1 teaspoon dried thyme
1 cup dry white wine

Trim the breast slices to an even shape and place in a wide saucepan with the trimming, the water, onion, celery, carrot, pepper and thyme. Add the wine. Simmer, partially covered, for 1/2 hour. Remove from heat and let turkey slices cool in their broth.

For the salsa:
1 cup Italian or flat-leaf parsley, chopped
1 tablespoon fresh tarragon, chopped
1 tablespoon scallions, chopped
1 teaspoon capers, chopped
1 jalapeño pepper, chopped
1/2 cup olive oil
2 teaspoons vinegar (from the jalapeño can)

Combine all ingredients and whip thoroughly. Let stand for 1 hour.

When ready to serve, arrange the turkey slices on a platter and top with the salsa. Serves 6.

TURKEY STIR FRY

A stir fry can be as simple or as elaborate as you wish to make it. The only requisite is a wok or large frying pan, ingredients cut into small pieces—to cook fast and evenly—and assorted flavorings. It must be served immediately.

1/2 cup peanut or safflower oil
1 clove garlic, chopped
1/2 cup red pepper, diced
1 cup broccoli flowerets
1 cup carrots, very thinly sliced
1 1/2 cups cooked turkey in either small slices or chunks
1/2 cup chicken broth
1 tablespoon soy sauce
1/2 teaspoon Tabasco sauce

Heat the wok or frying pan over high heat until a drop of water will sizzle and evaporate on contact. Add the oil and heat for 1 minute. Sauté the garlic until lightly browned. Add the red pepper, broccoli and carrots, toss well and cover the pan for 2 minutes. Uncover the pan, add the turkey, chicken broth, soy sauce and Tabasco, stirring constantly, until everything is heated through. Serve over rice or noodles. Served 4.

TURKEY KABOBS

Kabobs are always fun and dramatic to serve. All the preparation can be done ahead of time and the cooking can be either under the broiler or on a charcoal or gas grill.

2 pounds turkey breast cut in 1-inch chunks
1/2 cup olive oil
1/4 cup lemon juice
2 cloves garlic, crushed
1 tablespoon fresh herbs (basil, thyme, oregano . . . choose one)
2 large red peppers, cored, seeded and cut into 1-inch squares

Marinate the turkey chunks in the combination of oil, lemon juice, garlic and herbs for at least 1 hour. Drain, reserving the marinade. Alternate the turkey chunks with squares of red pepper on 6 large metal skewers. When ready to cook, place over a medium grill or under the broiler—about 6 inches from the heat—and cook for about 15 minutes, turning often and basting occasionally with the reserved marinade. Serve over a bed of rice. Serves 6.

VARIATIONS
1. Use squares of onion, half mushrooms and cherry tomatoes as the vegetables.
2. Marinate the turkey in a combination of 1 cup plain yogurt mixed with 2 cloves crushed garlic, 1 teaspoon black pepper and 1 tablespoon dried mint. Cook as above.
3. Alternate the turkey with partially cooked squares of bacon and firm prunes.

TURKEY MEATBALLS

These savory meatballs can be used as an appetizer, main course, party snack or an adornment to pasta.

1 pound turkey, ground
1/2 cup dry bread crumbs
1 medium onion, grated
1 teaspoon ground coriander
1/2 teaspoon ground ginger
2 tablespoons parsley, finely chopped
1/4 cup vegetable oil
1 egg, well beaten

Combine all ingredients in a large bowl and mix thoroughly. Let stand, covered, in the refrigerator for 1 hour. Form the mixture into small balls, about 1-inch in diameter. Handle lightly to avoid a stodgy, heavy end product. Now, you can sauté the meatballs in a non-stick skillet or you can poach them for a lighter texture and more delicate flavor. To fry, simply coat the skillet with oil and sauté over medium heat, turning often, until browned on all sides, about 15-20 minutes. To poach, half-fill a heavy skillet with water or half-white wine/half-water. Bring to a low boil, add the meatballs. Immediately turn down the heat to a very gentle simmer. Let poach, stirring carefully, now and then, until cooked through, about 15 minutes. Remove with a slotted spoon and drain. The meatballs can be served as they are with a mustard dip or with a light, spicy tomato sauce. Serves 8 as appetizers, 4 as a main course.

TURKEY SOUBISE

Soubise is the classic French sauce made of béchamel and pureed onions. It is perfect for a cold night when you need something both soothing and substantial. It's particularly good accompanied by crisp fired potatoes and buttered spinach.

1 pound turkey breast, cut in 1/4-inch slices
1/2 cup flour
4 tablespoons butter

For the sauce:
3 tablespoons unsalted butter
3 tablespoons flour
1 cup warm milk
1/2 cup chicken broth
1 medium onion, grated and blanched for 2 minutes in boiling water
1/4 teaspoon grated nutmeg
1/2 teaspoon white pepper

Dredge the turkey slices in flour and sauté in butter until browned on both sides, about 10-12 minutes. Keep warm. In a small saucepan, melt the butter over low heat, add the flour and stir constantly until well-blended. Let cook on low for 2 minutes, stirring all the time. Gradually add the warm milk, whisking constantly, until a smooth mixture is achieved. Add the chicken broth and the blanched, still-warm onion, the nutmeg and pepper. Continue stirring over low heat for at least 5 minutes, until the mixture begins to thicken and get glossy. Pour over the turkey slices and serve. Serves 4.

TURKEY CHILI

Everyone has his or her own recipe for chili, most being far more elaborate than necessary. Here's a quick-to-fix, low-cholesterol chili for entertaining or freezing for an easy meal at any hour.

4 tablespoons olive oil
2 large onions, chopped
3 cloves garlic, crushed
3 pounds cooked turkey, coarsely chopped
4 tomatoes, skinned and coarsely chopped
4 tablespoons chili powder
1 teaspoon ground coriander
1 teaspoon Tabasco
4 cups chicken or turkey broth
2 teaspoons ground black pepper
2 teaspoons salt

In a heavy pot, heat the oil over medium heat. Add the onions and garlic and sauté for 10 minutes, until lightly browned. Add the turkey, tomatoes, chili powder, coriander and Tabasco. Add the broth and mix well. Turn heat to low, cover the pot and simmer for 1 hour. Add salt and pepper to taste. Serve with beans or over rice, accompanied by chopped raw onion, sour cream or yogurt and a fresh green salad. Serves 8-10.

TURKEY PROVENÇAL

Provence, in the south of France, is a land of sun and olives, wild landscapes and warm, Mediterranean cooking. This dish uses the olives, tomatoes and garlic of the area to create something new.

4 tablespoons olive oil
1 1/2 pounds turkey breast, cut into 1/4-inch slices
flour for dredging
3 cloves garlic, chopped
1/4 cup dry white wine
1 pound tomatoes, peeled and coarsely chopped
freshly ground black pepper
1/2 cup black or green olives, pitted and roughly chopped
4 anchovy filets, chopped (optional)

Heat the oil in a heavy skillet. Dredge the turkey slices in flour and sauté over high heat, until browned on both sides. Remove to a platter and keep warm. In the same pan, sauté the garlic for 2 minutes, add the white wine and let cook down to half its volume. Add the tomatoes pepper and anchovies. Let simmer for five minutes. Add the turkey slices and the olives, cover the pan, and cook for another 10 minutes over low heat. Serve with buttered pasta and a green salad. Serves 4-6.

TURKEY SALAD

Turkey salad can be boring, but prepared this way, it becomes not a substitute for chicken salad, but a whole new experience.

4 cups cold, cooked turkey, cubed
1/2 cup almonds or pecans, coarsely chopped
1/4 cup onion, finely chopped
1/2 cup apple juice
3/4 cup mayonnaise
1 tablespoon lemon juice
1 1/2 teaspoons salt
1 teaspoon black pepper
1/2 teaspoon ground ginger

Combine the turkey, nuts and onions in a large bowl. In a separate bowl mix the apple juice, mayonnaise, lemon juice, salt, pepper and ginger. Pour the dressing over the turkey and toss well. Let stand for a 1/2 hour to blend the flavors. Serve on a bed of lettuce and garnish with black olives. Serves 8 as an appetizer or 4 as a main course.

CURRIED TURKEY

Curry is a good, quick standby. Quick to make, subject to infinite variations, it makes a complete meal along with rice and chutney.

2 tablespoons butter
1 large onion, chopped
1 clove garlic, chopped
2 heaped tablespoons curry powder or paste
1 tart apple, cored and chopped
1 tablespoon fresh ginger, chopped
2 cups cooked turkey, cubed
1 1/2 cups chicken broth

Melt the butter in a saucepan over medium heat. Add the onion and garlic and cook until soft and translucent. Add the curry powder and paste, mix well and let cook for 2 minutes. Add the apple, ginger, turkey and broth and simmer for 15 minutes. Serve over rice with chutney, chopped peanuts, grated coconut and chopped scallions. Serves 4.

Turkey makes light and healthful salads.

TURKEY BURRITOS

Fresh wheat tortillas make for better burritos if you can get them.

4 tablespoons peanut or safflower oil
1 cup onion, chopped
1 clove garlic, chopped
2 tablespoons chili powder
1 teaspoon ground cumin
juice of 1 lime
2 cups cooked turkey, roughly shredded
4 large wheat tortillas, warmed

Garnishes:
sour cream
chopped cilantro
chopped onion
guacamole
shredded cheese

Heat the oil in a saucepan. Add the onion and garlic and let cook until soft. Add the chili powder and cumin, the lime juice and just enough water to make a very thick paste. Add the turkey and just heat through. Place 1/4 of the mixture on each tortilla and fold up. Serve with some or all of the garnishes and refried beans. Serves 4.

TURKEY MILANESE

The most basic of Italian recipes, and one of the most satisfying. To be authentic, the cutlets should be fried in butter. Serve with lemon wedges and creamed spinach.

4 turkey cutlets
1 egg, beaten with 1 tablespoon water
1 cup fresh, dry bread crumbs
4 tablespoons unsalted butter

Place the cutlets, one-by-one, between sheets of wax paper and pound gently to flatten to 1/4-inch thickness. Dip the cutlets in the beaten egg mixture, then in the bread crumbs. Let sit for 15 minutes before cooking. Melt the butter in a large skillet over medium heat. Add the turkey cutlets and sauté for 5 minutes on each side. Turn up the heat and sauté another 2 minutes on each side to brown and crisp the outsides. Serves 4.

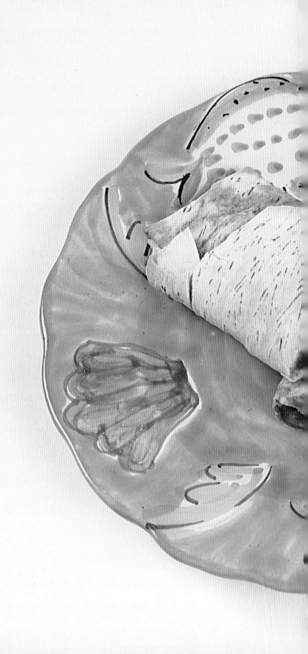